Less Obvious Gods

Less Obvious Gods

Poems

Lisa Coffman

Iris Press
Oak Ridge, Tennessee

Cover Painting:
Morning 2003
egg tempera on gessoed wood 48"x 36"
Copyright © by Sarah McEneaney
courtesy of the artist and Tibor de Nagy, NY

Book Design by Robert B. Cumming, Jr.

Library of Congress Cataloging-in-Publication Data

Coffman, Lisa, 1963-
  [Poems. Selections]
  Less obvious gods : poems / Lisa Coffman.
      pages ; cm.
  ISBN 978-1-60454-222-6 (pbk. : alk. paper)
  I. Title.
  PS3553.O412L47 2013
  811'.54--dc23
                                    2013009738

For Jaine Eileen Rice

CONTENTS

III: A Bestiary

IV: Always by That River

The Grebe

The wind beat its grand canopy of empty.
Breakers hammered a pitted ice color.

I turned to see the grebe make its way
dragging a flopped leg and wing

back to the water I had carried it from
wrapped in my coat. While I went for a box

—*misery* being my invention—
reptile cousin, red tattoo eyes, hissing beak,

I saw you reach a cold pane that slid under, lifted,
saw you swim out, get knocked under, knocked backward, swim.

And at last sit hunched on the shore, facing outward.
All day your weight has lingered in my hands.

What is near now stuns like your body's touch,
cold sea, flare of wings.

What is it to live wild?
Not separate from what you are ruled by.

I

ALL THAT SWAYING

TIME

We have called you fleeting
when we in fact are the brief ones.

We have said you steal,
when you could not have been more generous:
our clocks exhaust themselves
counting what you offer;
rocks crumble
before they are done being your ledgers.

From your vantage, our faces' deepening shadows
flicker sweetly as violets;
the oldest photographs
form with us a moving picture.

Therefore we name perfect
only that which withstands you.
Thus the bald-eyed statues
in the museum
staring wildly at rain,
thus the lines "but these words I command
are immortal."

And you, meanwhile,
who do not wait
for the other shoe to drop,
for the phone to ring,
have we not saddled you, lightest of bodies,
to carry the snagging burden of our longing?

Oh tombstones with little sepia photographs,
lovers burning to surmount you with one good kiss,
oh physicists who fix you with the four straight pins of coordinates,

and spots of the universe where you are said to run backwards
(that old trick of upending the hourglass)—
if you were less clear-souled, you might be amused.

How we miss what you are.
Most modest of the gods,
there is no monument you would let stand.

BASS

Down where you are
nothing breaks:

not the heart
not the voice

and the pedigree crystal
gets to go on shivering
with what you put in her.

I admit I began listening
only after a grief
stilled and dropped me
down through the melody
and exposed your great timbers,
your mineral dark,
the fine seismic pluck of your canter.

So I came to love the *mmmm* buzzing my lips
more than the taste of the frosting.
I came to love the shake of laughter
more than the joke that went before.

You're the shadow required
for each thing that flies
except your shadow throbs back into body
and we're touching by the time I hear you.

Like the pelvis that carries
the chalky dishpile of the spine
you carry harmonies stacked above you

and that is why
my hips love you best
and sway as though your
notes opened within them.

1

Pain

What are you, but trying to come through more clearly?
In bone or breath, or the incomplete called *soul*—
spaces too narrow for you to work in.

Though I could accuse you of being the narrow one
who crops things down to a few cruel words,
a fracture's shadow, a lonesome morning.

Did you ask to come in? I've felt complicit.
Could I make space enough for us to live comfortably?
Then you might not tear up where you're kenneled.

It must be embarrassing, the words I do find—
my lover dumped me, I write like shit—
that's where you struck, not what you are.
My letters grow plaintive. But what to ask for?

And allied against you—nearly everything.
Flesh's urge to mend, shame's to walk straight,
hospitals, the reign of heaven.
Monkey flower May through September.
It's a wonder you get through.

How is it you whittle me to the sole, the estranged one,
when your mark is everywhere?

COLD

Come November, you begin your work of turning us from you.
In the blurry pressure of your approach
you almost, and do not, take shape.
Such beauties as there are, you concentrate—
orange streaks in the sky at five,
the clarity of light signaled from windows.
In these, you set up evidence of your lack.
Color and fire are indoors, where you have driven us,
faces flushed above bright sweaters
among flowers tied and hung upside down to dry.
For abundance you have us resort to smaller and smaller measures.
Every meeting is a pact against you, a conspiracy of heat,
every conversation in a foyer—
"oh the tides that summer at Mont Saint Michel!"—
every group under a light at a table
who have come in from you and must go out again soon.
You sort us remorselessly, the way livestock is sorted:
the person sprawled under blankets on a sidewalk grate,
the person stepping around, who picks up speed.
Your intentions aren't clear. You take our breath, our one liberty,
and hold it up in front of us, painted white.

NOT CHOOSING OTHERWISE

Here they say "going to the snow." There we lay under it
as it came on. Without the trouble of choosing otherwise.
Let the heat of the rooms grow even oppressive
held within the generous, empty touch of cold
until we could bear a little of our own coolness,
stand naked in a room inside the snowing.
It limited our waywardness, as it did the tarry slide of rivers.
Muted the shapes of hills but retained them,
working as memory does, blessedly covering.
All day the slowness of it. The balked light.
A presence that would not spend itself in one impulse.
Or tears of the Virgin sent to anoint us
that cherished themselves on the way down and retained
remoteness even at the moment of blessing.
In my room under the roof, by the sleeping dog,
at my desk with a bird's nest brought in from summer,
and two horse bones that had worked their whiteness
out of the earth of the body
and then the earth where the body lay buried,
I typed small neat dark tracks on paper,
all of it open and slowly filling with snow.

talks to render

SMALL PAINTINGS WITHIN SARAH MCENEANEY'S PAINTINGS

Let me tell you about the house I just left—I would not tell you so
    leisurely if I still lived there—
two silver maples fill the back yard, their roots making it difficult to
    mow,
and a canal cuts across the yard's edge, below the towpath,
where the geese honking each morning sounded gearlike or archaic.

I worked by a window on the second floor, the plane of my desk high as
    the maples' branches.
I liked when rain or storms came during the day—the leaves slithered,
    the early dark was a kind of reprieve.
My desk overlooked a peeling side porch—since painted for the new
    tenants—

flanked on one side by red impatiens, the other by my garden
which I planted knowing I was leaving:
three kinds of tomatoes, peppers, marigolds to keep off bugs, petunias,
    snapdragons.
I wrote down each thing I planted and then let weeds grow up and
    choke it.

However, as my new friend pointed out, I planted mostly annuals.
She is a painter, she lives alone. I think she has a sense of completeness
    about her
like the interior of one of her paintings that includes even chair rungs
    and braiding in a rug.
She paints with egg tempera, her colors bright and also soft, like my
    snapdragons.

I have planted there, in other years, lilac, crepe myrtle,
a full-grown dogwood for the man I left, a butterfly bush for the child
    I aborted.
The summer of the abortion I bought for myself a bougainvillea, which
    flared and died after summer.

My friend's paintings record small details with a sort of faith, as a child's
    drawing does:
a calendar page has all its boxed-off numbers, a toy dog's penis
    has a pink tip,
lines of grout wobble between individual red tiles in a kitchen.

In a self portrait, she lies reading in bed
under a tent of mosquito netting. A window showing a moon is open.
She reads on her back, her legs straight, her arms bent and close
    to her sides.
Her fox terrier sleeps on an oval rag rug, both dog and rug curled
    similarly.

In a tiny painting on the bedroom wall of this painting, a man kneels
    before a woman.
Both are nude, he is shown from the back, from the waist up, the woman
    is sitting.

As he eats her, his thumb and forefinger form a circle at her nipple,
and her head, thrown back, shakes out her hair.

Just so, the small metal front of my oscillating fan picked up the opposite
    of what I saw
when I lay in bed a little too long in the morning,
as it swung from side to side of the flower-curtained room
passing over my head, surprisingly dark on the pillow, like a stranger's

or, when my lover murmured "pretty"—I was bent over the bed straight-
    ening covers—
the fan showed my short gown, ridden up, exposing my lower ass,
smudged double curve of vulva, a pale blue length of tampon string, and
    I bounded shyly off.

My friend did this for a time in her work, adding a small picture unlike
    its larger picture.
To identify a painting I ask about, she says, "What's the small painting
    in it?"

uses you

SECRETS

Room within every room.

Moon the horizon
is pressed to release.

Undeveloped, colorless

image exposed and gathering
in the necessary dark.

We like you, I think:
you rebuke the obvious;
you press upward
against what weighs down.
You prove every inventory
to have missed some thing.

No family occasion
turns you away.
Even between two people
you indicate which quiet
is counterfeit.

Oh treasure that cannot
be taken out and admired,
you know your worth
lies in the withholding—
your marked X more exotic
than the bauble it stands for—

yet you seek the surface:
pressure rising
the nearer you get

the way breath tears at a swimmer
the last instant before air.

I wonder, in your worst form, which is more terrible:
when you are uncovered or when you are never uncovered?

Room within a room
and then a partition.

Perhaps truth requires you
the way we do:
to make fools
of those who come nearest.

uses you

BALANCE

True, I have not desired you.

Nor what I perceived as your conditions:
the yardstick spine, the tightly laced ankles.
More applause when given less and less to stand on.

Nor that you leave me simply as myself,
going to and from the car with groceries.

Also true: beneath your even horizon,
an intimacy with the question-mark sway of the stack,
you who free every move by settling its cost.

But tell me where I find in you conflagration,
the thrill of aspiring, the kiss that lays low.

Meanwhile you go on tending me
      —myriad adjustments even while falling—

LETTER TO MAJOR RAGAIN WITH A FEATHER
FROM ATASCADERO BEACH

Maj, This kissed the Pacific.
Godwit, I think: the long, improbable
dental-instrument-thin bill graced the birds nearby.
It ought to tip them. (See Sibley's *Guide to Birds*,
whimbrel through curlew.) I tip, going to the surf,
my longboard one blade of a mostly stuck windmill.
Once in, sometimes I fly—
feet strangely planted in a crescendo roar,
the breaking apart shooting me forward.
More often I'm knocked off, legs above head
(the pose that liberates), then sprawled
with what the wave does below the wave.

The fear that closes over me is not like that:
it has no pour, no surfacing once I'm under.
I was trying to outwalk it when I saw the feather,
its dark bands, the plump comma asymmetrical shape.
I thought I might take it for my study—
I admire studies with things like that.
And isn't it fine, the way the halves don't match?
The bands on one side heavy, over dramatic,
the others zagging off to nothing, data dots, static...
thin graze of layer adding up to mark the bird.

And then (I should have known this would happen)
I couldn't pick up the feather, couldn't
just pick it up and put it in my pocket.
I walked off a little and came back,
walked off with everyone walking, and came back,
and stopped, the weight piling on my breath—

That was the week Margaret said, calmly,
as if directing me to reach something for her off a shelf

which, on crippled days, she had to do,
"If you black out, your breathing will resume.
You will start breathing."

I thought, *I'll give Maj the feather,* and put it in my pocket.
After that it was easy enough to take a sand dollar;
a hole broken in the top showed through sand crust I brushed off.
But the beautiful double-frond pattern of the sand dollar picked up
    beyond the hole,
looking inked on the bleached surface, with the tiny exclamation-strokes
    of Vincent van Gogh.

It moves me, these things keeping to what they are,
the broken part against the part that's kept.

The sand dollar is on my desk, trickling sand near the computer key-
    board.
And here is the feather.

And I am like the people I see hiking to Third Street lookout
where birds wheel in great flocks or come settle on the bay.
And to this, the lightest, finest thing, these hikers carry
and stumble under clumsy tripods and scopes.

LIGHT COMES AT ME SIDEWAYS

> I never live with balance
> I always wake up nervous
> Light comes at me sideways
> I hold my breath forever
> —Bruce Cockburn,
> "Open"

Tuesday sun laid on, I write, but it's Thursday
(and oh God the puppy's dug up the yard).
When I called the banjo *holy,* I meant
walks beside all things: creek in sun, walnuts
hitting a tin roof—it's light's hold on water,
it's the way the apostrophe holds the *s*
not too close, a good dancing partner.
Or that the fallopians don't first touch the egg,
but fringe it over: they could be adder heads,
a Venus Fly Trap, I hope not, but anyway,
isn't all that swaying in the name of embrace?
Sometimes I stray so and tangle in metaphor
I end up making love to the wrong thing,
B rather than A, my own pleasure in manufacture.
And why I like tangent better than pilgrimage:
no posted lookout, no time to arrive,
the best place to taste the lover's mouth.
For whenever did desire strut down the avenues
in full dress like a marching band drum major?
Ah, the coyness of those summer screen doors—
the air stirred through, a figure darkening close—
greatly open without seeming so.

II

THE OTHER BODY, IRIDESCENT

BLACK RADISH

In January, in cold soil, the radishes
are not secretive
although they might be
accused of that.
Why else the remote
white of star
in that complete dark?
Why else the brilliant mask
of plum, of rose?
The ones called icicle,
pulled from the ground,
are wound warmly together.
The green radish, cut,
reveals a plum flare
like a startled bird.

Under their disregarded greens
the radishes are plentiful
and come up easily for us.
And within the flesh:
a fanning of white on white,
delicate as a bride.

They are so other
from what we say they are
they might as well be hidden.

Too, can we blame them
for delivering the sharp
retort, the peppery edge
only after initial mildness—
which of us has not done that?

The hesitant among us
hide them in salads;
those who can stand back talk
eat them in wedges with a portion of salt.

Best of all, this January
I stood above the cold beds
cutting radish after radish
next to the thin farmer who grew them
and ate, trying to miss the dirt

until we came to the black radish,
whose inner white
is most soiled, whose skin
has the surly color
of tire marks

and in her sharpness
I forgot former tastes,
in the way a difficult
love is most difficult
to stop loving. I had to chew
the other, milder radishes,
many of them,
to get back to that obsolete sweetness.

There Is Something Lonely about the Warmth of a Coat

Used to, when I put on my coat and scarves you were there.
It was a gesture—we did not need such warmth.
Now I put the coat over a terrible hurt
and wrap it tenderly around this body you have said *no more* to.
I go to tell the women.
With their wise kind eyes they take me in
with whatever else they take in in the distance.

uses you

Some Honey

You are the measure of Laphroaig scotch
the beekeeper hid in a quart of raw honey,
heated then cooled into the amber.
The shudder of hard sugar down in the sugar.
What the news of smoke does to the sweet.

A ROYAL COACHMAN TROUT LURE SENT AS COURTSHIP GIFT

Miniature aggressor in tinsel, tippet, fluff,
perched so lightly on my hand
the hook doesn't prick.
(If I blow a kiss, it flies.)
Lets my finger stroke its wings—
folded up, as if for take off—
wings snipped from mallard feather
and the coppery hairy body
wrapped in peacock herl
that vaguely makes me squirm.

I have to say "I'm touching it"
to feel a thing at all.
(In herl alone a warning:
the feather carries barbs.)
Next, floss, wound tight, like I am,
and splayed pheasant-tippet tail.
For he is so bold, this love who sent it,
that he declares his recipe for the lure.
"There's something godlike," he writes,
"in selling these illusions."

Lure patterns have names like Humpy,
Stimulator, Wooly Bugger. The Royal Coachman
isn't meant to imitate a real fly
but provoke a strike
from fish not used to being pressured.

Imagine the cast! The clear water wicking
up past hook to the barely alighted body.
Then the other body, iridescent, rising.

uses you

KISS

Before buttons and unbuttoning,
before the lock fell to the key
or the prelude gave away parts of the opus

you had your practice, an adept,
you kept your X'd map of our coordinates

you went on setting your little traps of pillows.

I can't flatter you sufficiently:
your indecent shine (like glimpsing a zipper),
your tongue loosing words off what they cover.
In broad daylight you smack of the ample bed
over a truck hood or luncheonette table.
I'd have been so upright without you—
kinks all still in my spine—
and no touching faith in the seasonal.

Naughty: the lines you blur but won't erase.
Tan line, lip line, language of a contract.

Strewn softness swamping the tooth,
balm to the wound, and wound giver, and wound,

you won't let us pretend
wet belongs to the other element.

ADORATION

Oh fire's mirror. God watcher.
Patron of the nuance:
shorts tightened
across a buttock
during the long stride,
graze of knuckles
when handing a drink.

And the quick weather of the lips:
how well you register
the lick leaving more wet,
the tooth mussing
pillowy plump,
the shape of the word and not the word.

Which god offers
better terms for love?
Which saint
such a postulant's approach?

What finer instrument
for measuring nearness
than your slow
indoor
hothouse spread?

Yet I must name
your failings,
mirror,
mirror:
you lack depth
and get things backwards,

confusing the pilot
with the sky
one who visits the Amazon
with the Amazon.

Like Southern California's stasis weather
you birth stage sets.
Working mostly at a distance,
you make things
billboard size.

Oh most yokel of emotions,

Oh god,
Oh god,

I think you're lonely.

INGREDIENTS

The winemaker said, "grapefruit... fresh pineapple" then "soil"
and whatever he said I tasted afterward in the clear glassful.
He tossed the rest toward a long grate at our feet
and strode off over it.
"The wine in these two vats are sisters, a year old, still cloudy."
"Why soil?" I said. "Ah! the young Chardonnay.
It is like a dirt road in rain, this taste of the dust.
Or a fresh loaf broken, and steam off the crust."
I tasted. But it was you I saw:
sprawled, broken, huge. Rain splotched your torso,
pocked pinkish dust, bore up a smell of dirt and salt,
and a pair of lovers lay facing each other, dissolved—
"Eh? You taste it, I think." "I do," drained my glass—
dissolved to dirt path, embrace braiding the surface.

THE PRINCIPLE OF TRANSFORMATION
AT A CADILLAC ANGELS SHOW

The scroll crested over the double bass turns into
the pompadour hairtop of the lead guitarist.

All the hearts, briars and stars inked onto soft arms
weep black tears their mascaraed girls can't cry.

The bar sleeve-worn past varnish gets sanctified
as dance floor under the hailstorm of Tony Balbinot's boots.

But the double bass, under the bassist's hands,
(he wrapped around, face pulled up close,
part embrace, part toppled together)
as he pats her to wails, hums, abrupt low chuckles,
flurries up and down her tight-strung flung-on-him weight
little strokes and smacks, stiff jiggled finger, the slide,
stirs her so she can't hold back any note—

the double bass doesn't turn into anything.
Every woman there wants to turn into her.

TRUTH

In the world of the quickly changing
only you, Truth, would I have unbrothered.

I assign you a marble reserve, a fixity.
I remove you from the thrilling ballyhoo of wind and ocean.

I have you say no to many things, to drive up your value.

Possibly you have layers, like the ocean's cold.
Possibly versions of you go farther

the way more postage sends letters to farther-flung regions.
But, as with all gods, I permit you two kingdoms:

the Absolute Somewhere (vacuum's ingot of light,
the cold aimed atom, the Greenwich standard)

or the Absolute Nowhere ("what people believe
in order to go on doing what they're doing,"

as when I write "I love him more than anything"
and love more than him just to write that statement.)

Of course the light shifts. Wind, branch, something wheeling—
the day's light that laid itself down now shatters

on the rosemary, the dazed bees,
ripples shadow quick as water on my white wall.

You're there, aren't you? Struck, spangled, refigured,
knowing to make yourself out of change.

To do so is in your survivor's nature.

Everybody Made Soups

After it all, the events of the holidays,
the dinner tables passing like great ships,
everybody made soups for a while.
Cooked and cooked until the broth kept
the story of the onion, the weeping meat.
It was over, the year was spent, the new one
had yet to make its demands on us,
each day lay in the dark like a folded letter.
Then out of it all we made one final thing
out of the bounty that had not always filled us,
out of the ruined cathedral carcass of the turkey,
the limp celery chopped back into plenty,
the fish head, the spine. Out of the rejected,
the passed over, never the object of love.
It was as if all the pageantry had been for this:
the quiet after, the simmered light,
the soothing shapes our mouths made as we tasted.

III

A Bestiary

Comma

Comma, half swish, quick skirt, catch for rest,

falling through the two elements:
above, the world of words, below, an uncertainty.

Leaned against the sentence's current,
against the straight line no thing can keep traveling,

with you I begin, *If God were not jealous,*
or I stay caught in *my love, my love, my love,*

With you, *The dog moves across the study,*
lies down, sighs.

Gentlest yoke, who hold apart with your pause,
    (the word just said still in the air)

dose of quiet, not absolute, not final,
a sip, a taste of the still, of nothing at all.
A little oar into the underworld.

CALF

And when the forelegs unlaced and let go,
when the little beads of hips slid, and the skull
foreshortened of hide seemed nearly human

still I came stitching myself under the fence wire
to crouch by the bright, wrung hide
by my galoot dog openly crunching the teaset-sized bones.

The calf died the way it slept
curled around the charm mound of its head,
one leg folded, one pointing a clean pink hoof forward.

More faithfully than to any god, we came:
the carrion eaters that persist past cringing
to pull the body a little way farther in dark,

the buzzards bulking up nearby trees,
and I bowing and straightening through fences
to watch the face in its sequined slide of flies

until the jaw in the long grass
waned, was the last thing lost. And the grass,
tossing and tossing it, was the jaw.

TICK

Harpoon-lipped wicked French kisser,
you near-do-nothing fattening
at someone else's board. How come
no heart beats all that blood, heat drop,
ballooned thirst, all lust? If our lives
are wrought by curse, who thought up yours
and for what crime? You do not ask
not to be hated, but approach
with galley-slave rowing motion
to your stubble legs, your slowness
not from indecision, not fear.
You'll scale the biggest predator,
risk a six-figure inflated
desk-bound mammal same as the cur
he's just kicked, and grip your beachball
bodied mate, a mangey hide bed
as good to you as my white skin
for fornication. You'd bite God!
Not daunted by coagulant,
not ashamed to hide your head
in rusty rivers everyone shuns,
you spit cement instead of fire,
a neat eater for a glutton.

Homely stigmata non grata,
we are not spared the cruelty
of mashing you with a brick edge,
a letter file, or, with tweezers
holding you to the thin match flare
until you pop. You do not go
easily, but ride the toilet's
tipped flush, upright as a captain
around and around, out of sight.

A wasp dangles legs delicate
as kite tails, the spider crochets
circular doilies, why do we
see in you nothing to admire,
nothing of ourselves? Heat seeker,
the places sweet to us are sweet
to you: neck, waist, the feathery
clefts of the crotch, taut soft hinges
where you plunge, hang head down, succumb.

OLD MORRO BAY AQUARIUM

Starts, as such worlds do, with gaudy heaven,
turquoise no ocean would force
on T-shirts, silver minced into keychains.
Mug fronts plead *I love… I love*
and one uncoastal snowman's stranded
tunelessly in his windup globe
since Only Store Personnel May Touch.

The real silver begins with chopped minnows
dampening the concessions bag
pushed through a cutout window sliding shut
once the gift store is left for good.

Two sea lions guard this passage.
Behind their chain-link fence they blare for fish
slap their backsides like strippers
and make all the cleverer children cry.

The aquarium itself is an honesty
of sorts—no light, no plate glass that disappears,
no ecstatic mailed bodies lifting out of sight.
Cold, glassy, dimmed, the place keeps
the ocean's terms for being entered.
Tanks flicker like projector screens
that reveal the pop-eyed bored or interrupted
where a moray eel bloats from pipe
and fish hang, aimed like signs.
A horseshoe crab, armored for nothing,
marches across its wastes.

"Look," a child calls. "Look, they are babies.
They have no feet."
A shark lunges through the stinging air
lacquered out of any atrocity.

A whale's jarred eye
peacefully loses its iris like a moon.

The old god, hauled in,
exhausted, tethered, slightly out of date,
still divulges what we've come to see,
what we think we're not.
Here, sex is tinkered with
(wrasses turning, in chorus,
male at age four),

and escape is nearly possible by peeping,
as with the octopus: "Intelligent as a house cat,
it can slip through any crack,
limited by the size of its keen, complex eyes."

Ranch Sapphics

Deep Springs Ranch, California

The business

Neither bulls nor male gynecologists seem
pleased enough. Listless as eunuchs, our bulls haul
sun-sized balls, mope. One bull—envied by ranch hands—
tripped on his penis.

Former butcher, steer calf

"He was down—clean shot to the head—I'd slit his
throat. He stood up. Threw me. This tiny, concrete
bloodied room, him coming at me. I ran. He
lived till I came back…"

First-year heifers adoring virgin bulls newly turned in with them

drop off romping. Wiggle, with high-heeled mall girls'
new-moon hips, in tipsy ellipses. Back right
up to the bulls, who back up, trip, freeze: strobe-lit
boys on the dance floor.

Cow

Goddess eyed, moon crowned, O our seven-stomached
suitcase-uddered blueprint for birth! Cut down, you
flower milk, placenta, brave calves. You clothe the
ranchers who curse you.

VOLLEYBALL PLAYERS AT LAGUNA BEACH

Women who hold their mouths around straight pins
to kneel at a hem line,
women who glare *boob job*
at hoisted cleavage,
women who *get* boob jobs,

do they get to be these women, centered
in spectators and sand,
women wearing so little without dancing?

And this isn't a triptych, either,
although the boardwalk preacher thinks
little hell flames lick the scene.
"Buddy," he cries to the man motioning to him *quit*
"if that's your wife out there, I pity you.
I'm not looking, Buddy. I'm preaching straight ahead."

But if gods are obsolete,
why sky and strike like a god
a toy ball one woman can wrap
entirely in her restless animal hand?
Or, if a god, why submit to tiny suits
that must not slip past tampon strings,
why deny body hair
except the faint glint
above trunks shucked just below the hips?

The women turn their wrists up to the ball's hurt,
they scramble under, hectic supplicants.
Slammed in sand, they do not cry
like men, nor, winning, hoarsely riot. They are remote
as Diana or the Fates, but more polite.

Only the boardwalk preacher knows
the old heart-coursing words *glory*   *Sweet*
Redeemer   *lust*
and he swears he's never looked.

Summer Solstice

Center pole raising
the greatest tent,
curtain drawn back farthest,
sum to which mathematicians
cannot put $+ 1$,
to which the child
cannot say "and then what"——

in a world of answered
desire, all days
would be like you.
And how happy, your clownish act
of keeping the sun
up so long, spinning.

No one thing can fill you:
not women weeping
as they lay out a body,
not the sand that scours,
not the ocean's silver.
You offer us time
to find out what really happens
after the solemn promise
or the once-and-for-all forgiveness.

All the other days stand
so that you may stand out among them,
the way the beloved
cannot be missed in a crowd.

And of you, whose reign
is most enlightened,
there are those who complain
that you announce more darkness

than any other,
that you herald
the long decline.
But I know
you are only
wonderfully intent
on keeping the sun suspended—
a trick you have mastered
so that your riches are weightless.

PASTEL CON TRES LECHES

Cake of three milks!
Threefold deity of the tit,
white banner of every infancy!
In your unstinting spill of light
we are again roundest and most loved.

White layer throwing no shadow,
white that no virginity
can ever tarnish,
you take back through your prism
all the ways milk
helplessly gives itself:
under the weight of sugar,
heated to exaggerate
cream's stain,
frank stream the penned-off calf
bawls for. Also you offer
a necessary taste of the sour
for the lush tears of childhood,
for the Madonna, whose heart
is circled with swords,
who goes on forgiving.
Every Wednesday
in one-room Taco Temple
under the hands of Dawnelle,
who must love us as you do,
who adds some days
the modest blush
of strawberry puree,

you take your place
on the dessert stand
across from the finite Pacific.

Ass

What I thought and where I went
(with you propelling) and the story I put to it—
all edited by the parentheses you swung.

Pleased jut while I've scrooged about having nothing.
Fine, hewn animal to my numbers-screwed brain.
If my heart's been hard, you advertise
(a parting shot) that *you're* a soft touch.

What amount of pin stripes got you to straighten?
Which sodden goodbyes haven't you clowned behind?
You play your kickdrum rhythm all my lonely walk to the car
after a lecture on TS Eliot has gone flat.

Civilization got you to sit still and look what it built:
caste and class act
numbers men totting up tithes to the king
scribes in library carrels
going on and on about swarthy heroes
and joyous dogs called sharply to quit sniffing

while you lob Russian dancers into endless ballon
while you tuck drowsing lovers against each other
while you get bared to the outhouse chair
and deal with the honest, messy nature
of when inner is brought forth to outer.

In the milky tremolo of a titty world
you've been my good end,
my ballast, my escape-velocity weight.

(As when he declared his love
at a party, in a side room, where we might've kissed,
I turned instead, backed into him.)

LISA   COFFMAN

"The subject of a poem is as foreign to it and as important, as his name is to a man."
—Paul Valéry

My two names
show up for a while around people I don't know.
Out on the periphery, they stay trained on me
like binoculars or a loyal dog.

Called out, they grant me passage,
perhaps with a smattering of applause,
to the front of an auditorium's shiny fidgets and coughs,
or to the head of a third-grade class, to read my poem on a squirrel.

Weeks go by and I may not hear them both.
They are like a skirt and shirt I wouldn't wear together
that turn up side by side on a clothesline to dry.

Without my two names I cannot owe money,
give an answer at a border
or lie under a grave stone.
I suppose I have come to blame them for this sort of thing.

We share a flawed loyalty: they remain
indifferent to any change on my part, any redemption.
They intend to outlast me, while I
will betray them at once for "my darling" or "mama."

We have gone on so long like this
in the dentist's waiting room, on the job application,
the book jacket, the church Christmas play program.

Today my friend brought a poem about an orange,
such a poem! its mist and rind hung in the air after we shared it.
I heard him say, as he left, "Lisa Coffman, sail on"

though now he claims he said "Lisa see-saw" and staggered off howling.
The point is this: I turned to my names with such hope.

I think I am still listening for my mother's voice.
I think I turn out of that portion of love which is obedience
and therefore never sure if it is love.
I turn quickly because now I protect her,
I turn toward her the part of me my names never covered.

Past Tense

Past tense, you bring near, you set next to me
what is not.

Such as *This morning, I got up, fried eggs, walked the dog.*

I like your light stride across a sentence.
I like the shadow you throw: first phase of an eclipse
in which objects grow not darker but richer.

Sometimes, when I am quiet, alone in my house,
I hear you come into the thing I'm doing.

Where Akhmatova writes "On the copper shoulder of the Lyre player
a scarlet bird sits," you are secretly there.

It is to you I turn for the kiss in the garden
and not the one who kissed me then.
In you, *in the last days, her appetite came back.*
She called for pork chops, a plate of greens,

It is with you I bind all my possessions
to carry the way of all possessions.

She said, "When I was a girl we never had a care.
We kept the babies all morning in the morning air
                    in white carriages.
Grandfathers on the stoops rocked them."

IV

ALWAYS BY THAT RIVER

BORN UNDER THE SIGN OF

You came in under the Vacancy light of my hotel-sign heart,
under the spearhead of my brash and undivided hips.

Now when I wheel down, with the other constellations, to rest,
you give me such a poke and shove, school-bully stuff

you can't have meant it.
Nor the way you crank up my ribs, a thief getting in a window.

Math can't account for us, neither one nor two
nor any of the numbers for in-between:

one of us standing, the other lying down,
one making fists, the other typing full sentences

and sometimes we face opposite ways, like opponents in a duel.
When they marqueed you on the sonogram screen,

when they said, as in an indictment, *there's the brain,
heart's all right, spine lips feet kidneys*

I saw you were already packing to leave,
neat valise of your head and chest

filled with the rolled and folded things you'd need.
Still, the hand I lay on you is laid on me,

the kindest hand I've had for myself.
Rocking soothes us: a motion made of *go* and *come back.*

Object Permanence

My girl has become encumbered by things
that go on being behind the sofa
or after the shut door. The grief of things
so burdened, so stooped with their primary colors
their ordinal processions, their ur-shapes—star,
bow, the bow's arrow, hunter—these crowd the night
and she cries. Once I came and went,
milk smear of light, noise and heat
that throbbed her sky, and each time I left
it was a good death, the way of things,
a dark-light-dark. Then a new death came.
Now she cries for me in the next room
for the light way I lay my hands on things
for the tiny wings I carry of my parents' deaths
for the small smile pinned to me, for my exact eye color
and that I wear black in summer, and that I hurry.

THE SHAPE OF LETTERS

"Try this," she says. I've said "not now."
I'm on the toilet. She stands, knees at my knees,
hand cupped around her lips. "Say *ffff*,"
she puffs it, *ffff, ffff, ffff,*
getting up a rhythm like the engine
that was brave, and made it over the hill.
"Feel that?" she says. "Say *hhhh*."
The dandelion light of her thin hair
rays in all directions, her eyes
above the cupped hand hold mine
the way she did before we had words.
"*Hhhh*," I try it, "*hhhh*." Against my hand—
too light, quick, gentle, damp for what I am,
too eager to rush past and spend its warmth—
breath accompanies the hard grid lines
of F and H, the tired, formal shape
made to stand all day and know some thing.
"Now *mmmm*," she says, "try *mmmm*."
And though my lips are pressed,
a little heat works out,
a freshness you would have to
fall to your knees near the thing
to register, or go close as this, cupped hand,
a secret to myself. Light warm quick gentle damp.
From my lips as from hers.
What I've been saying with whatever else I said.

THE BEES

What is whole lacks compassion.
Before I learned this I heard the bees.
The hive's voice is the voice of an old god
broken among many. In this way, singing.

My House, Summer '98

Sometimes I see things the way Sarah McEneaney might paint them.
This morning, for instance, the blinds were out of their usual rigor:
      they squiggled like toothpaste.
I saw that my husband and I, lumpish in bed, betrayed,
      in the hollow of a chest or cheek,
some fertile human darkness blooming through,
while our hands and knees, tucked under pillows or each other,
      signaled small, almost secret, signals of comfort.

This has happened since I watched Sarah mix egg tempera.
She sludged pigment into the spilt yolk;
      the runny color gave itself over to the new color
the way, when we walked into Sarah's neighborhood,
it gave itself over to one of her paintings.
I saw veins rivering an old man's hands
above the powdery orange that ate his stoop railing.
In beaten lots, weeds floated various yellows
among the vague cheer of colored letters
      naming broken cans and glass.

I saw even myself, at the bottom right of a painting,
later, as I sat with Sarah in her garden.
I liked looking in on myself from that distance,
with my shirt pulled sideways where I'd slid in the chair
and a light frost smudging my raised glass of scotch.

Then I remembered a real painting of her garden.
My House, Summer '98.
Sarah sits alone, shown from the back,
the garden's neat, swept and weeded, with new tomato plants in planters.
She's reading, one hand rests lightly on a hammer.

Her newspaper carries the words of the man who broke in that summer:
SHUT UP I'LL KILL YOU SHUT UP WHERE'S THE MONEY SHUT UP YOU
    KNOW WHAT I'M HERE FOR I'LL KILL YOU KISS ME BACK

I thought, stupidly, Sarah had said once
a detail like dots for snow might take several afternoons.
Then I saw her painting those words
alone, in her studio, where, she had told me
with two yolks probably she could paint all day.

LOST SONG

If we could blast all pity from love!
Like clearing the smell of an infection from a room...
or like a comfortable woman, lax from napping under blankets,
who slips a spoon of sweet batter to a child in red pajamas.

Well, I wish I could talk for my heart, as Vallejo does.
I wish I could share my heart like bread.
But it has not been amiable: it grieves only for me;
if I lie awake at night, it fears only for me.
I think it has been too faithful
like the suffering face depicted for the Virgin—
No, it is an ordinary heart, roosting in me
like a bird singing, that forgets it is singing.

LETTER TO MAJOR RAGAIN:
THURSDAY PAINTERS AT ELFIN FOREST

Maj, Yesterday I walked the boardwalk that loops through Elfin Forest.
Strung along the walk was a group of painters
each painting the bay toward Morro Rock,
an immense rock out in water bare of any explanation.

I would have liked still another painter
to do this landscape of Ten Painters Painting
in their spindly archipelago of chairs and easels
and palettes mucked in bright lizard colors
and fussy manicurist gestures over each Rock's picture.

I noted, as I passed, the exuberance of watercolor,
which exceeds the line it is asked to declare,
and the reticent oil paint, with its stormed-in surface.
Eleven times I passed Morro Rock on that walk.
Eleven times I was given the opportunity to practice
the David Ignatow poem you read to me this week:

> I should be content
> To look at a mountain
> For what it is
> And not as a comment
> On my own life

(I loved, by the way, your kind voice intoning "end"
to mark where each poem line stopped.
This became a new poem over that poem.)

Eleven times I failed at the practice.
For no mountain has commented on my life,
and I wouldn't know which version of the Rock to pick
so I could see it for what it is.
As the painters showed me, sometimes the Rock is swollen purple,

or scrawled darkly with lichen.
Or it may hold more sky alongside it,
or be pale as a dove, or sunk low in the water.

Listen, Maj, what if none of us can ever be looked at
for what we are? Oh, I would be content
to walk always beside that marvelous river
of ten painters who move to a new scene every Thursday
and reflect for each thing its tenfold image.

BEGINNING

How rarely now, Beginning,
do you strew your pure salt taste through my days!
How rarely do you consort with me anymore
to bring me again to my shyness,
to the working of my hands.
Today at the bass lesson
in a room small enough for whispering,
small enough for trysts,
I sat down with a stranger
(for you come only to strangers)
who set my hands on the bass,
who had me pluck each string alone
for what seemed a long time
to bring it around to its note.
This, before any music.
Who, other than you, Beginning,
requires that I go completely on faith?
How far off you stand from everything finished—
from everything you alone open toward.

Once I play a song in that room, will I notice
any more what I noticed with you:
the cartilage of the frets
the space between strings
I looked at instead while my teacher named the strings?
The hesitancy of my hands at new touch that felt like hurt?
All the things—the carpet of the room, the shoes—
that had nothing to do with what I came for?
You leave me tender, helplessly seeing,
the way only grief does, or departure.

Once in my days I know you were everywhere.
Now I come to meet you by way of task:
ruled, with notes or scales to learn,

or the house-shaped letters of a new language.
But as soon as there is a track, a pattern,
that is as far as you take me; you have left me already!

Perhaps I am too rough, damaging you, and that is why you don't last.
No: you are the one thing truly unknowable,
offering no second chance. You are that harsh a lover.

Cumberland Spring

1

Nights, I sit up too late.
In the morning, with what relief
I begin at one window,
watching only the old apple tree,
the small distances of birds changing branches.

2

Pony bones and jonquils in the yard,
vertebrae flared like the jonquils.
My peace is with these sunning bones.
It arrived, I never did get to it.
What was all that, beforehand, for?

NOTES

The quote in "Time" is a fragment from Sappho, translated by Mary Barnard.

In "Truth," the quote is a paraphrase from Robert Penn Warren's "The Circus in the Attic": "people always believe what truth they have to believe to go on being the way they are."

My observation in "Tick" that "a mangey hid bed" is "as good to you as my white skin/for fornication" was brought on by this information from Roger Drummond's *Ticks and What You Can Do about Them*: "Adults find hosts, suck blood, and mate... Mating usually takes place on the host before feeding."

The quote that ends "Old Morro Bay Aquarium" accompanied a 2006 exhibit at that aquarium.

In "Past Tense," the lines quoted for Anna Akhmatova are a paraphrase from her poem beginning "I can still see hilly Pavlovsk," translated by Judith Hemschemeyer.

The David Ignatow lines quoted in "Letter to Major Ragain: Thursday Painters at Elfin Forest" are from Ignatow's poem "I Should Be Content."

ACKNOWLEDGMENTS

I thank the editors of the following magazines and online journals in which these poems first appeared:

Aperçus Quarterly: "Light Comes at Me Sideways," "Not Choosing Otherwise," "The Past Tense," and "Lisa   Coffman"
Artful Dodge: "Everybody Made Soups"
The Beloit Poetry Journal: "Small Paintings within Sarah McEneaney's Paintings"
Cafe Solo: "To Cold"
Eat This Poem: "Black Radish"
Meridian: "Tick"
Mid-American Review: "Calf"
Pennsylvania English: "Lost Song"
San Pedro River Review: "Born under the Sign of," "Principle of Transformation at a Cadillac Angels Show"

In addition to appearing in *The Beloit Poetry Journal,* "Small Paintings within Sarah McEneaney's Paintings" has been anthologized in *A Fine Excess: Fifty Years of the Beloit Poetry Journal.* "Tick," which initially appeared in *Meridian,* has been published in the anthology *Listen Here: Women Writing in Appalachia.* "Time" was published in the 2012 *Jawbone Book* commemorating the annual Jawbone Poetry Festival in Kent, Ohio. "Kiss" and "A Royal Coachman Trout Lure Sent as Courtship Gift" have been published in *Myrrh, Mothwing, Smoke: Erotic Poems.* "Cumberland Spring" is forthcoming in *The Southern Poetry Anthology, Volume VI: Tennessee.*

I want to thank my husband Joe and daughter Jenna for their steady love and encouragement during my various weathers as a writer. I'm also grateful to Major Ragain and the holy-roller Jawbone crowd for keeping alive my love for poems. Kevin Clark, James Cushing, Peter Everwine, Michael Hannon, Michael Hobbes, Margaret Mehring, Don Morris, Alicia Ostriker, Linda Patton and Dian Sousa offered needed support and advice as I put together this manuscript. I'm also grateful for Bob Cumming's editorial suggestions in the home stretch and for Beto Cumming's fine eye as a book designer. Finally, I thank Sarah McEneaney for letting me use one of her remarkable paintings for my book's cover.

CPSIA information can be obtained at www.ICGtesting.com
Printed in the USA
LVOW12s2101081013

356020LV00001B/12/P